The Fun Fashion Show

by Sam Gayton
Illustrated by Emma Levey

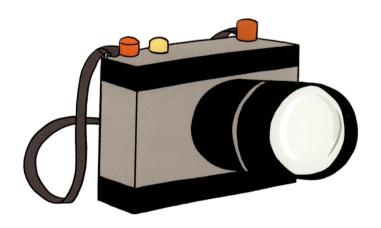

OXFORD
UNIVERSITY PRESS

In this story …

Pip and Kit run *Finders Squeakers* — a lost and found agency. They help return lost things to their owners.

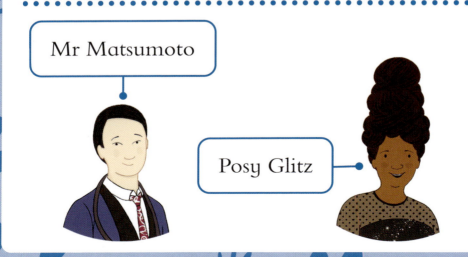

Chapter 1
Let's go!

Pip grabbed her motorbike helmet and put it on. "Let's go, Kit!" she said.

Kit looked up from his cat bed. "Huh?" he said, with a yawn.

Pip started the motorbike. "We have a *Finders Squeakers* mission!" she exclaimed.

"Grab that suitcase, please, Kit," Pip said.

"Are we going on holiday?" Kit asked.

"No!" replied Pip, giggling. "We need it for the mission."

Kit squeezed into the sidecar.

With a screech of tyres, they shot off.

"Where are we going?" asked Kit.

"To the Funky Fashion Show," Pip yelled, over the roar of the engine.

"Wow!" Kit replied. "What are we going there for?"

"We need to find a lost camera," Pip explained.
"Mr Matsumoto is a photographer. He has come
all the way from Japan to take pictures of the
show, but his camera has gone missing!"

"That sounds like a job for us!" Kit said.

Chapter 2
Posy Glitz

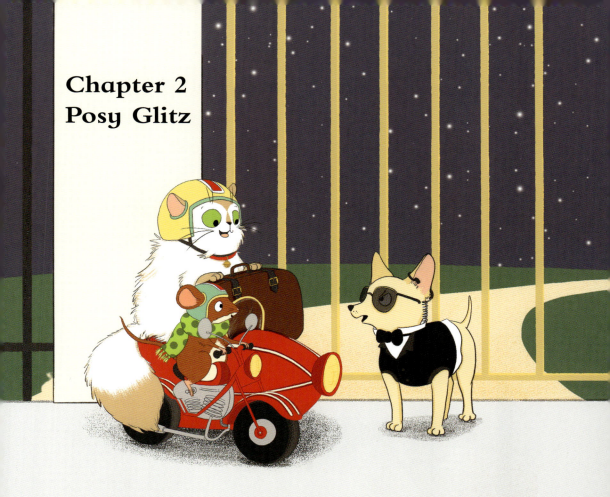

Pip stopped by some enormous golden gates. "This is it!" she said.

"Can I help you?" yapped a guard dog.

"We're here for the Funky Fashion Show," Kit said.

"You don't look like you are," growled the guard dog. "Go away!"

Pip parked the bike around the corner, where the guard dog couldn't see them.

"How are we going to get into the show now?" Kit said. "We need a plan!"

Pip opened the suitcase. "Actually, I already have a plan," she <u>admitted</u>. "That's why I brought these." She pulled out two outfits.

When you <u>admit</u> something, you confess that you did it. What has Pip <u>admitted</u> on this page?

Kit gasped. "Great idea, Pip! We won't get into the Funky Fashion Show unless we look … well, funky!"

They quickly changed into their outfits.

"I like your cape," Kit said.

"Thanks!" Pip replied. "You look *pawsome*."

Pip and Kit hurried back to the gates.

The guard dog didn't recognize them in their outfits. "Welcome to the Funky Fashion Show," he yapped as they entered.

The show was in a huge glass building.

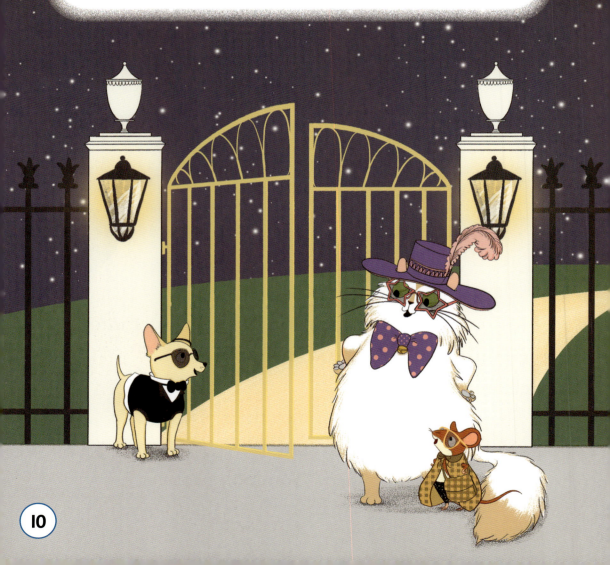

Inside, the rooms were full of people. The whole fashion community was there. Models were walking up and down the stairs, dressed in every colour of the rainbow.

Pip and Kit hurried through the crowd, looking for the lost camera.

A community is a group of people who have something in common. What do you think the people at the show have got in common?

Pip spotted a tall woman on the stairs. "That's Posy Glitz," she said to Kit. "She's the most famous model in the world!"

Posy Glitz's hair had been shaped into a tall tower for the show.

Kit's eyes went wide. "What an unusual hat she's wearing!" he said.

Pip got out her binoculars. "That's not a hat. It's … a camera!" she said. "We've found it!"

"I wonder how it ended up there?" Kit said.

Pip looked up at the balcony above the staircase. "The camera must have fallen off the balcony when Mr Matsumoto was up there," she said. "Then it must have landed on Posy Glitz. Her hair has been piled up so high, she probably didn't feel it land. Now everyone thinks it's part of her outfit!"

"How will we get the camera back?" Kit wondered.

"I'm not sure. Everyone is looking at Posy. We'll be spotted at once!" said Pip.

"We need to distract everyone," Kit said. He looked at the catwalk where the models would show off their outfits. A plan began to form in Kit's mind.

Why does Kit need to form a plan? What has helped Kit to form his plan? What did he look at?

Chapter 3
Catwalk

Kit explained his plan to Pip, and they both hurried backstage. Pip found the switches that turned on the lights and music.

"Good luck, Kit," Pip called, flicking every switch on. "Do your best!"

Kit leaped on to the catwalk. He struck his funkiest pose. Then he walked to the end of the catwalk and did a <u>double</u> spin.

Everyone fell silent. Then someone shouted: "Ooooh! A cat on a catwalk!"

All of the photographers rushed over to the catwalk. At once, their cameras started flashing.

Kit did a <u>double</u> spin on the catwalk. Does this mean he spun round twice or three times?

No one was looking at Posy Glitz any more. This was Pip's chance. She scampered up the staircase, then slid down the banister like it was a giant slide. With a great leap, Pip landed on Posy's towering hairdo.

Meanwhile, on the catwalk, Kit strutted backwards and forwards. As he posed, more and more fashionable figures came to watch him.

Kit did another spin.

A figure means a person. Describe one of the fashionable figures at the Funky Fashion Show. What are they wearing?

Pip grabbed Mr Matsumoto's camera. "Got it," she said to herself. "Now I just have to get down."

Just then, Pip had an idea. "I hope this will work," she thought.

Pip took a deep breath, then … jumped!

Pip held out her funky cape and used it as a parachute. She floated back down. Then she ran through the crowd until she was safely outside.

Everyone cheered and clapped as Kit strode out of the show.

"Kit!" Pip hissed. "Over here!"

"We did it!" Pip said to Kit, holding up the camera. "You were brilliant on that catwalk!"

Kit was unable to hide the huge grin on his face. "Thanks, Pip," he said. "I wish all our missions could be as funky as that!"

The next day, Pip and Kit got a message from Mr Matsumoto.

Please accept two tickets to next week's Outrageous Outfits Fashion Show as a thank you for returning my camera.

Do you think Kit and Pip will accept the tickets to the Outrageous Outfits Fashion Show, or do you think they've had enough of fashion shows?

Read and discuss

Read and talk about the following questions.

Page 8: Can you describe a time when you <u>admitted</u> something to a friend? How did it feel?

Page 11: Teachers and teaching assistants are part of the school <u>community</u>. Can you think of anyone else who is part of the school <u>community</u>?

Page 15: Can you describe the last time you <u>formed</u> a plan?

Page 17: Can you think of something you might want <u>double</u> of and why?

Page 19: What did the fashionable <u>figures</u> think of Kit's catwalk performance?

Page 23: How did you feel the last time you <u>accepted</u> a gift or present?